EYES ON
INSECTS

Ruth Strother

Silver Dolphin

Silver Dolphin Books
An imprint of Printers Row Publishing Group
A division of Readerlink Distribution Services, LLC
10350 Barnes Canyon Road, Suite 100, San Diego, CA 92121
www.silverdolphinbooks.com

Printers Row Publishing Group is a division of Readerlink Distribution Services, LLC.
Silver Dolphin Books is a registered trademark of Readerlink Distribution Services, LLC.

All notations of errors or omissions should be addressed to Silver Dolphin Books, Editorial Department, at the above address.

Written by Ruth Strother
Designed by Haydee Yanez

ISBN: 978-1-68412-315-5
Manufactured, printed, and assembled Heshan, China. First printing, May 2018. HH/05/18.
22 21 20 19 18 1 2 3 4 5

Image Credits: The University of Texas at Austin, Insects Unlocked Project, Getty Images

CONTENTS

WHAT IS AN INSECT?

You might think you know what an insect is, but do you really? Some people think spiders are insects, but spiders are arachnids. One difference is that spiders have eight legs whereas insects have six legs. Some people think that roly-polies (also known as pill bugs and woodlice) are insects, but they're crustaceans. They're more closely related to shrimp and crabs than they are to beetles! So what makes an insect an *insect*?

• All insects have six legs, and instead of bones insects have a hard outer shell called an exoskeleton. Most insects also have wings and two antennae.

• All insects have three main body parts: a head, a middle section called a thorax, and the end of their body, which is called an abdomen.

• All insects begin life in an egg. Some hatch out of eggs as nymphs and look like smaller versions of adults. They molt, or shed their skin, several times until they're all grown up. Others hatch out of eggs as larvae, which often look like grubs or worms. Larvae enter a stage called metamorphosis. During metamorphosis, the insect, now called a pupa, is wrapped in a cocoon or a chrysalis. When the insect breaks out, it has changed into its adult form. Butterflies are the best-known insect that goes through metamorphosis.

Scientists estimate they know about 900,000 different kinds, or species, of insects. But they think there may be millions more that have not yet been discovered. Let's take a look at the amazing variety and some of the mind-blowing traits we can find in the insect world today.

SWEET
BLUEBERRY BEE

Bees are the little delivery vans of the insect world. Each time a bee drinks nectar from a flower, its powdery pollen gets picked up in the bee's hairs. This is called pollination, and pollen is one of the ingredients flowers use to make seeds and fruit.

Blueberry bees are so good at pollination that farmers invite as many bees as they can to their blueberry fields. They do this by building nests for the bees out of blocks of wood. Farmers aren't afraid of having a lot of blueberry bees around because these sweet bees hardly ever sting!

INSECT INFO

Scientific Name:
Osmia ribifloris

Native Range:
Arizona, Arkansas, California, Oregon, Texas, and Utah

Non-Native Range:
Alabama and Mississippi

DID YOU KNOW?

Blueberry bees live alone and do not build hives.

STINGING SOUTHERN YELLOW JACKET

The southern yellow jacket is a wasp that fiercely protects its queen and paper-like nest. When disturbed, guard wasps swarm out of their huge underground nest to attack. Although these wasps drink nectar, they also eat other insects. They use their stingers to poison their prey.

Looking more like bees than wasps, southern yellow jackets live in backyards and in parks. You can see worker wasps hovering around garbage looking for food, and they are often uninvited guests at picnics. They're not just looking for food for themselves. They also take food back to the nest to share with others.

DID YOU KNOW?

Up to 5,000 southern yellow jackets can live in one nest.

INSECT INFO

Scientific Name:
Vespula squamosa

Native Range:
Canada: Ontario
US: From New York to Florida and Iowa to Texas
Mexico: Chiapas and Tamaulipas to Michoacán
Central America: Guatemala and Honduras

SUNFLOWER-LOVING LONG-HORNED BEE

INSECT INFO

Scientific Name:
Svastra obliqua

Native Range:
Southern Canada, United States south through Central America

DID YOU KNOW?

A queen either lives in a nest with her young, or the nest is like an apartment, where each queen has her own entrance to her private part of the nest.

A bee with horns? Of course not. The name comes from the long antennae that decorate the male long-horned bee's head. The females don't have long antennae, but they do have really hairy legs! Sometimes their back legs look like fuzzy yellow cowboy chaps because they get covered in pollen.

Long-horned bees play favorites when it comes to the flowers they pollinate. Sunflowers are the bee's knees for these buzzers. A female long-horned bee takes pollen from flower to flower to help them make seeds. She brings leftover pollen to her underground nest to feed her young. Next time you eat sunflower seeds, you can thank the long-horned bee.

SINGING

ANNUAL CICADA

You may not know what a cicada looks like, but you've probably heard one. The loud buzzing you hear in summer is likely a cicada's song. Only the males sing, though. And they don't sing from their mouth—they sing from their bellies!

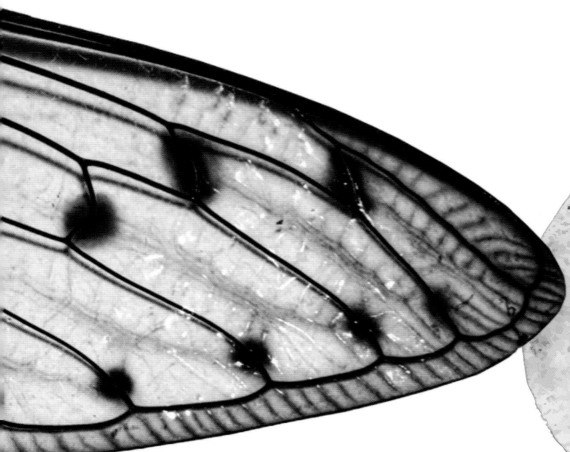

DID YOU KNOW?

Annual cicadas appear every year, but some cicadas spend up to 17 years underground.

A male cicada's abdomen is mostly empty except for two organs called tymbols. Muscles squeeze and release the tymbols up to 400 times a second to make the cicada's vibrating song. The swelling, earsplitting buzz of cicadas can be louder than an airplane's engine! That's because the empty abdomen acts like a drum and amplifies the sound.

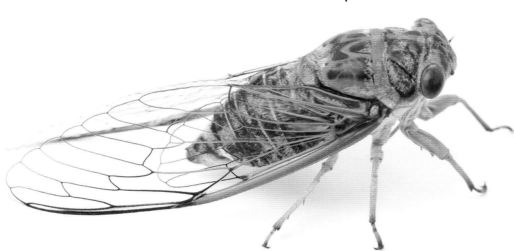

INSECT INFO

Scientific Name:
Neotibicen spp.

Native Range:
Canada, United States, and Mexico

BUMBLING GREEN JUNE BEETLE

The shiny green June beetle bumbles across yards, flying in search of overripe fruit. As it sucks juices from the fruit, this beetle drips liquid from its body. The liquid leaves an awful smell and taste on the fruit. It's not surprising that green June beetles are considered pests among fruit growers.

Their young, called grubs, are pests that live underground. They eat grass roots, often destroying yards and golf courses. When they get older, they shimmy to the surface. Stiff little hairs help them walk. Surprisingly, the hairs grow along the grub's top. Green June beetle grubs walk on their back!

DID YOU KNOW?

Female green June beetles fly just above the grass in the early morning; males fly in the mid to late mornings.

INSECT INFO

Scientific Name:
Cotinis nitida

Native Range:
Eastern United States

The female glowworm beetle doesn't look like a beetle at all. She looks more like a worm. In fact, she looks like her young in the larva stage. Her body is made of segments. Every segment has a spot on each side that lights up. Some even have a light-up band between each segment. The larvae can glow, too, and so can the eggs. But it's lights out for the males.

The male glowworm beetle doesn't glow. He looks more like a typical beetle, except for his feathery antennae. This is more than decoration. The antennae help males "smell" females when it comes time to mate.

DID YOU KNOW?

Glowworms are most active at night. They glow to warn their enemies that they taste bad.

INSECT INFO

Scientific Name:
Phengodes spp.

Native Range:
Southern Canada, through the United States, to Chile

SHINING GLOWWORM BEETLE

DID YOU KNOW?

Sweat bees can be plain looking, but many kinds have shiny metallic green or blue coloring.

INSECT INFO

Scientific Name:
Halictus spp.

Range:
Worldwide

THE LITTLE SWEAT BEE

It's not by accident that sweat bees buzz around people on hot summer days. These common bees are interested in the salt in human sweat. They hover around us, hoping for the chance to steal a taste. It's a good thing it takes a lot to make them sting. And when they do, their sting is not very painful.

These little bees are important pollinators. Hundreds of different kinds of sweat bees visit all types of flowers. They don't make honey, though. The female brings pollen to her underground nest. She places it next to her eggs to feed her young when they hatch.

HOLE-PUNCHING LEAFCUTTER BEE

When it comes time to lay eggs, the female leafcutter bee becomes nature's hole punch. But her targets are leaves, not paper. The punched-out leaf circles are used to make a nest almost anywhere she can find a narrow, hollow place.

She lays an egg, makes a ball of pollen and nectar for the larva to eat when it hatches, walls it off, and repeats 12 to 40 times.

The leafcutter bee gets pollen and nectar from all the different crops and plants it pollinates. Instead of trapping pollen in leg hairs, like the honeybee does, leafcutters trap pollen in the hair on their bellies.

DID YOU KNOW?

The biggest bee in the world is a leafcutter bee called Wallace's giant bee. It has a 2-inch wingspan!

INSECT INFO

Scientific Name:
Megachile spp.

Range:
Worldwide

BITING MOSQUITO

INSECT INFO

Scientific Name:
Family Culicidae

Range:
Worldwide except Antarctica and Iceland

DID YOU KNOW?

Mosquitoes cause more diseases than any other animal in the world.

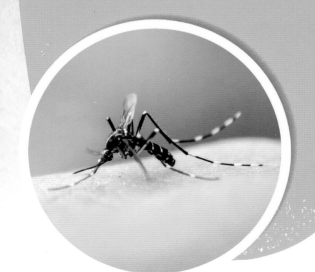

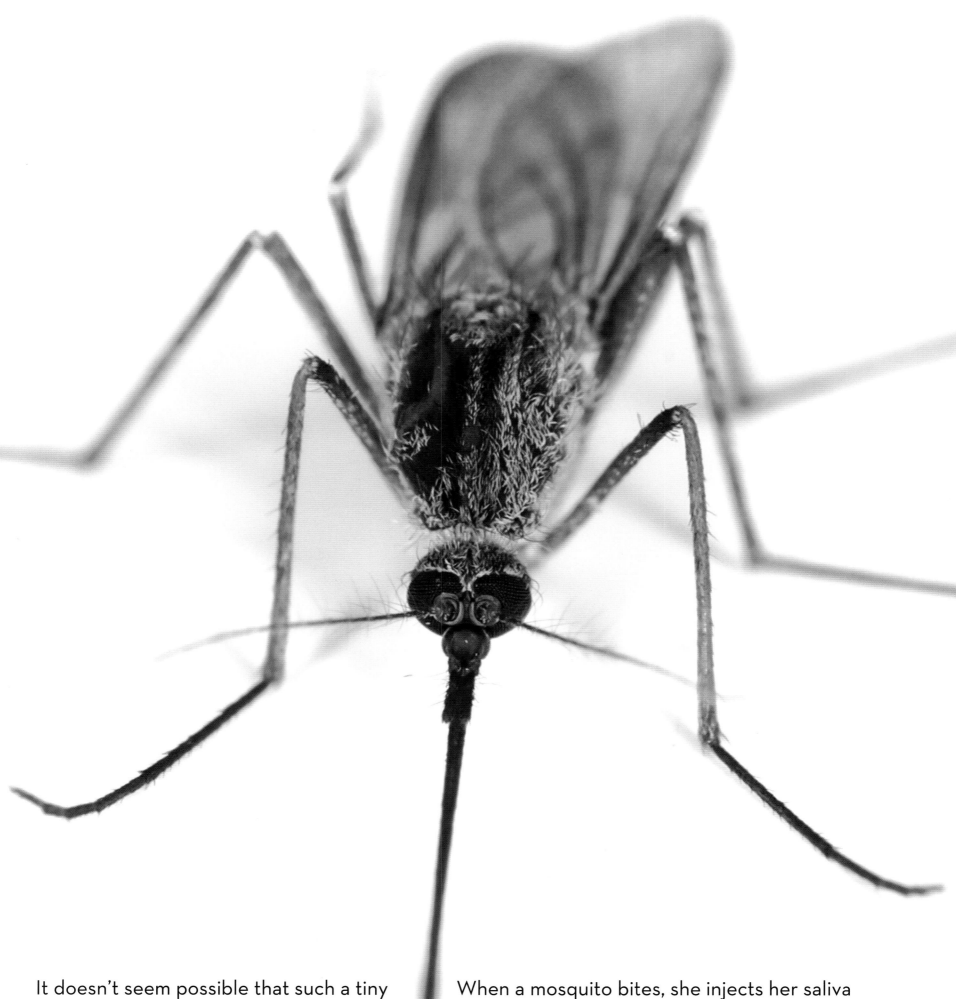

It doesn't seem possible that such a tiny creature could cause so much trouble. But mosquitoes spread some of the worst diseases to people. Only female mosquitoes are guilty of this, though. Both male and female mosquitos drink nectar, but a female needs blood for her eggs to grow. She gets that blood from humans.

When a mosquito bites, she injects her saliva into her victim. Germs hitch a ride in the saliva of some mosquitoes, and that's how diseases are spread.

The saliva keeps blood from clotting so the mosquito can suck it right up. And the red, itchy bump you get is an allergic reaction to her saliva.

THE WOOD-CHEWING

WESTERN CARPENTER BEE

One of the biggest bees in California, the western carpenter bee looks like a black, bald, fat-headed bumblebee. They're called carpenter bees because they chew perfectly round holes in wood to make their nests. Sometimes the wood is part of a house, fence, or a newly dead tree.

Each female western carpenter bee builds her own nest. She defends her nest, but only if there is great danger. She's not quick to sting, but when she does, her sting is painful. The males, however, don't sting, and western carpenter bees are known as the gentle giants of bees.

DID YOU KNOW?

When they can't get into a long, narrow flower, western carpenter bees will bypass the pollen, bite a hole through the flower's base, and suck out the nectar.

INSECT INFO

Scientific Name:
Xylocopa californica

Native Range:
Oregon, California, Utah, Nevada, Arizona, Texas, and Mexico

THE DEADLY BEE ASSASSIN

INSECT INFO

Scientific Name:
Apiomerus spissipes

Native Range:
Central United States

DID YOU KNOW?

The bee assassin's bright red-and-yellow coloring is a sign that it doesn't taste good, so predators stay away from them.

Hiding among petals, the bee assassin is ready to ambush its next meal. When a bee lands on the flower, the bee assassin attacks. Its front legs are equipped with sticky hairs that help it grasp the bee. Then the bee assassin injects its beak into the bee and pumps special saliva into it. The saliva keeps the bee from moving and turns its insides to mush so the bee assassin can drink up.

Bee assassins attack useful bees, but they also attack insects that cause damage to plants. That makes it hard to tell whether bee assassins do more harm than good for our gardens and crops.

EYE-FLASHING IO MOTH

With a wingspan of up to three inches, the large Io moth is speckled brown, red, or yellow. These moths usually live in forests with leafy trees. Their color is perfect for blending into fallen leaves, where they rest during the day. It's at night that they go flitting about.

This moth has a big surprise—two big surprises, really. For protection, the Io moth spreads its wings to show off two eyespots. Its predators fear that the "eyes" belong to an animal that might try to eat them! Io moth caterpillars don't have eyespots. Instead, they protect themselves with black, poison-tipped spines.

INSECT INFO

Scientific Name:
Automeris io

Native Range:
Southern Canada, eastern United States, Mexico, and Central and South America

DID YOU KNOW?

Female Io moths lay a cluster of up to 35 white-and-yellow eggs. They can also lay hundreds of eggs during their brief lifetime.

MIGRATING MONARCH BUTTERFLY

Millions of monarch butterflies fly a 1,500- to 3,000-mile migration between their summer and winter homes every year. But not all monarchs make the trek. This bright and cheerful butterfly gives birth to four generations a summer. It is the fourth group that gets to travel.

As caterpillars, monarchs feast on poisonous milkweed plants. The poison doesn't harm them, but it stays with them even as they transform into butterflies, and it makes them taste bitter. The monarch's signature orange, white, and black markings are a warning to its predators.

DID YOU KNOW?

Monarch Butterflies use their antennae to "smell" and their legs to taste!

INSECT INFO

Scientific Name:
Danaus plexippus

Native Range:
Mexico, United States, and Southern Canada

SHIMMERING BLUE MORPHO BUTTERFLY

INSECT INFO

Scientific Name:
Morpho peleides

Native Range:
Central and
South American
rain forests

DID YOU KNOW?

The flutter from blue to brown of a morpho's flight makes it seem to disappear for a moment. A handy trick when being chased by a predator.

One of the largest and most striking butterflies in the world is the blue morpho. From wing tip to wing tip it is eight inches wide. With wings folded, the blue morpho is brown and blends into its surroundings. But opened wide, its wings are a shimmery, bright blue. Morphos aren't really blue, though. They look blue to us because they are covered in tiny scales that reflect blue light.

Blue morpho butterflies spend much of their life near the forest floor. But when it's time to find a mate, morphos flitter around the treetops, showing off their blue wings.

THE FLY-AWAY-HOME LADYBUG

The ladybug most of us know is the seven-spotted ladybug. In the 1900s, these ladybugs were sent from Europe to the United States to help farmers get rid of pests called aphids. To this day, ladybugs are welcome in gardens and farmland for the same reason.

Ladybugs come in many colors and patterns. Their bright colors warn predators that these pretty little beetles taste awful. But if a bird or other enemy still tries to eat them, ladybugs "bleed" a terrible-tasting oily liquid from their legs. If they dodge predators and make it through the summer, ladybugs gather in large groups to hibernate through the winter.

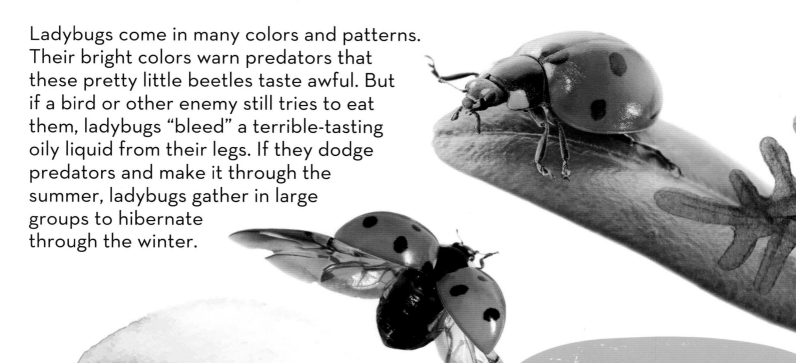

DID YOU KNOW?

NASA rocketed ladybugs and aphids into outer space to be studied.

INSECT INFO

Scientific Name:
Coccinellidae septempunctata

Native Range:
Europe and Asia

THE ANCIENT

More than 300 million years ago, dragonflies measured two feet from wing tip to wing tip. Today, the wings of the biggest dragonflies span just five inches. It's no wonder that dragonflies are skilled fliers. Each of their four wings moves on its own, allowing dragonflies to fly in any direction. They catch their prey with their feet as they fly. Dragonflies can eat hundreds of mosquitoes in one day!

But dragonflies spend most of their lives in water as larvae—sometimes up to five years! They eat other insects and even fish. When they leave the water as adults, dragonflies live no longer than a few weeks.

DRAGONFLY

DID YOU KNOW?

A dragonfly's eyes are so big that they cover almost all of its head.

INSECT INFO

Scientific Name:
Suborder Anisoptera

Range:
Worldwide

THE MAGICAL CATERPILLAR

DID YOU KNOW?

The stages of metamorphosis are egg, larva, pupa, and adult.

INSECT INFO

Scientific Name:
Larva in the order Lepidoptera

Range:
Worldwide

Caterpillars are young butterflies and moths, and they are expert eaters. They hatch on a plant and start munching, often devouring every leaf. As they grow, they shed their skin, a process called molting. Then one day they stop eating. That's when a caterpillar's life goes topsy-turvy, and the "magic" begins.

Using their rear legs and a bit of spun silk, caterpillars attach themselves to something solid, such as a twig, and hang upside down. They either spin a cocoon or molt into a chrysalis. After a few days, they break out of their wrappings all grown up as butterflies or moths.

39

SCURRYING AMERICAN COCKROACH

Cockroaches have been around for more than 300 million years. After all that time, it's no accident that more than 5,000 different types of cockroaches scurry across the earth. These insects are skilled at fitting into almost all conditions.

We see cockroaches as a sign of filth and disease. But only a tiny percentage, which includes the American cockroach, carry germs. These critters are active at night and eat almost anything in our homes, including glue. They dart over garbage looking for food and picking up germs. A cockroach can live one month without food, two weeks without water, and more than one week without its head! Keeping cockroaches away is one of the best reasons for keeping a clean house.

DID YOU KNOW?

To reach its maximum speed of 3.5 mph, the American cockroach has to run on just its hind legs.

INSECT INFO

Scientific Name:
Periplaneta americana

Range:
Worldwide

INSECT INFO

Scientific Name:
Family Scarabaeoidea

Range:
Worldwide except Antarctica

DID YOU KNOW?

Dung beetles are good fliers and use their antennae to "smell" dung from the air.

THE ACROBATIC DUNG BEETLE

The dung beetle is all about poop. These little beetles dig into it, eat it, lay eggs in it, and roll it around. Some dung beetles form dung into a ball, get into a "handstand," and push the ball backward with their hind legs. They need to get it to their nests quickly before the dung dries out. They can't see where they're going, so they use the sun, moon, and stars to know where they are in relation to their nests. Dung beetles are the only insects that use the Milky Way to help them navigate. Once at home, the dung beetle buries its ball and uses it as food and a nursery.

THE STINGING

Don't be fooled by the fuzzy velvet ant. Although you may want to pick it up and pet it, watch out! This is not an ant. It's a wasp. The males have wings and look more like typical wasps. But the females don't have wings. Instead, they have an inch-long stinger that delivers one of the most painful stings in the insect world.

The sting isn't the only form of protection the female velvet ant has. Her outer shell is so hard that predators have trouble biting into it. And when attacked, she makes squeaky sounds that startle her enemy. Her bright colors are a warning to predators to stay away.

VELVET ANT

DID YOU KNOW?

Some velvet ants are called cow killers because people think the pain of a velvet ant sting is so strong that it could kill a cow. Luckily, the pain of the sting only lasts thirty minutes.

INSECT INFO

Scientific Name:
Dasymutilla occidentalis

Native Range:
Mexico, United States, and Southern Canada

THE UNDERGROUND RAINBOW SCARAB BEETLE

Who would think that such a bright, colorful, and shiny beetle would spend most of its life on, in, or under poop? The rainbow scarab beetle is a dung beetle. But instead of rolling a dung ball to their nests, rainbow scarabs just dig in. They dig tunnels in the ground below a heap of dung. Then they roll up little balls of dung. The female lays an egg in each dung ball and places each one in its own tunnel. Not all tunnels are nurseries, though. Some tunnels store food balls made of dung, and some rainbow scarab beetles stay underground for months, hiding from winter.

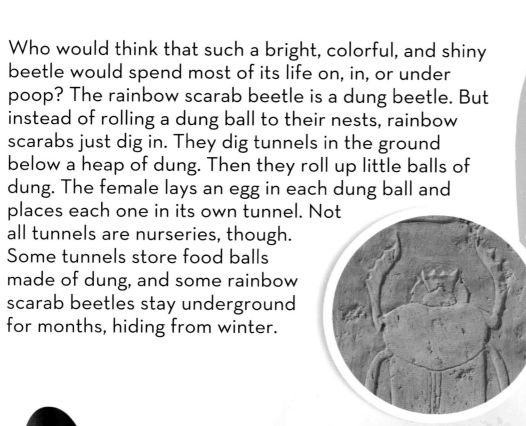

INSECT INFO

Scientific Name:
Phanaeus vindex

Native Range:
Eastern United States from South Dakota to Massachusetts in the north, and from Texas to Florida (except for the Everglades and the Florida Keys) in the south

DID YOU KNOW?

Ancient Egyptians worshipped scarab beetles. They collected the prettiest rainbow scarab beetles and made them into jewelry.

THE MYSTERIOUS TEXAS IRONCLAD BEETLE

Not much is known about this ancient-looking beetle. But we do know how it got its name. Its exoskeleton, or shell, is iron-hard and difficult for predators to bite into. But this isn't the only way the ironclad beetle keeps from being eaten. Its striking white-and-black coloring makes it look like bird droppings, something predators are not likely to eat. These beetles also play dead. When touched, the ironclad beetle tucks in its legs and doesn't move for a very long time. As much as ironclad beetles seem like knights ready for battle, they are harmless to people and plants.

INSECT INFO

Scientific Name:
Zopherus nodulosus

Native Range:
East central Texas, and Northeast Mexico

DID YOU KNOW?

A hard shell covers its wings, making it impossible for this beetle to fly.

49

BUMELIA BORER BEETLE

The bumelia borer beetle is a type of longhorn beetle. Instead of horns, though, it has really long antennae. This beetle is called a borer because its larvae bore, or dig, into the roots or wood of dying trees. And the adults are often found on bumelia gum trees.

It's exciting to come across this 1.5-inch shiny, green beetle with its bright-orange legs. This jewel of the insect world is hard to find, though. Bumelia borers are a bit skittish. When one is disturbed, it releases an odor that tells all the other borers to run for cover.

THE GEM-LIKE BUMELIA BORER BEETLE

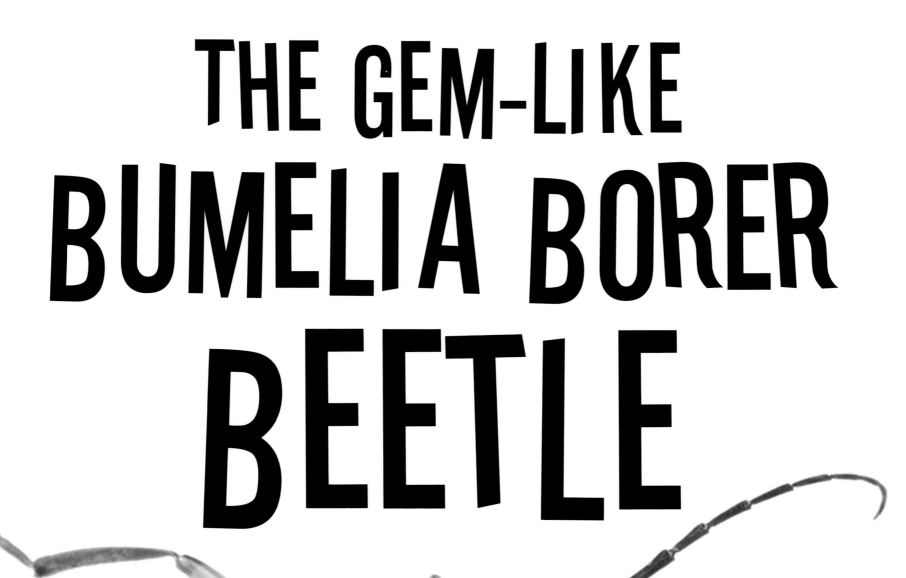

DID YOU KNOW?

The larvae often bore into tree roots and emerge as adults. Adult males are often found facing downward on trunks, waiting for females to appear.

INSECT INFO

Scientific Name:
Plinthocoelium suaveolens

Native Range:
Southern United States

THE PHANTOM STICK INSECT

Stick insects, also called walking sticks, are masters of disguise and mimicry. They are usually green or brown and look more like twigs or leaves than insects. Most of their days are spent hanging under plants. They become more active, munching on leaves, once the sun goes down.

Blending into the background isn't a stick insect's only defense. Some stick insects have wings that they spread to scare away enemies, and some might pretend to be dead or squirt predators with toxic juices from their body. And if an enemy happens to nab a leg, stick insects can grow a new one!

DID YOU KNOW?

One type of stick insect stretches out to be 22 inches, making it the longest in the insect world.

INSECT INFO

Scientific Name:
Family Phasmatidae

Range:
Worldwide

INSECT INFO

Scientific Name:
Cephalotes spp.

Native Range:
North America, Mexico, and Central America

DID YOU KNOW?

As with other social insects, such as other ants and honeybees, each turtle ant has a special job to do.

What in the world would an ant use such a huge head for? Your imagination can go wild, but the answer is pretty ordinary. Turtle ants use their large head as a door. Any ant wanting to get in or out of the nest needs to get the guard ant's permission. And it's not likely that an intruder would get past this armored gateway.

These ants live in trees. Some types of turtle ants use their oversize head as a parachute to soften their landing if they fall out of a tree. Some can even glide back up to their nest! When they fall, turtle ants can stretch out their body and limbs so they don't fall head over heels. They twist in the air and point their abdomen in the direction they wish to go, and glide backward at a steep angle.

THE BIG-HEADED TURTLE ANT

THE SMELLY STINK BUG

There's no mystery as to why these insects are called stink bugs. When threatened or crushed, these shield-shaped critters release a horribly smelly aroma that some describe as smelling worse than dirty feet. The stink is not just to chase enemies away. It also lets other stink bugs know that danger is near. Strangely, the stink helps these little bugs attract their mates!

Stink bugs have piercing mouthparts that they use to suck up juices of fruits and other plants, often ruining whole crop fields. But they're not all bad. They also suck up the juices of other insects that destroy crops.

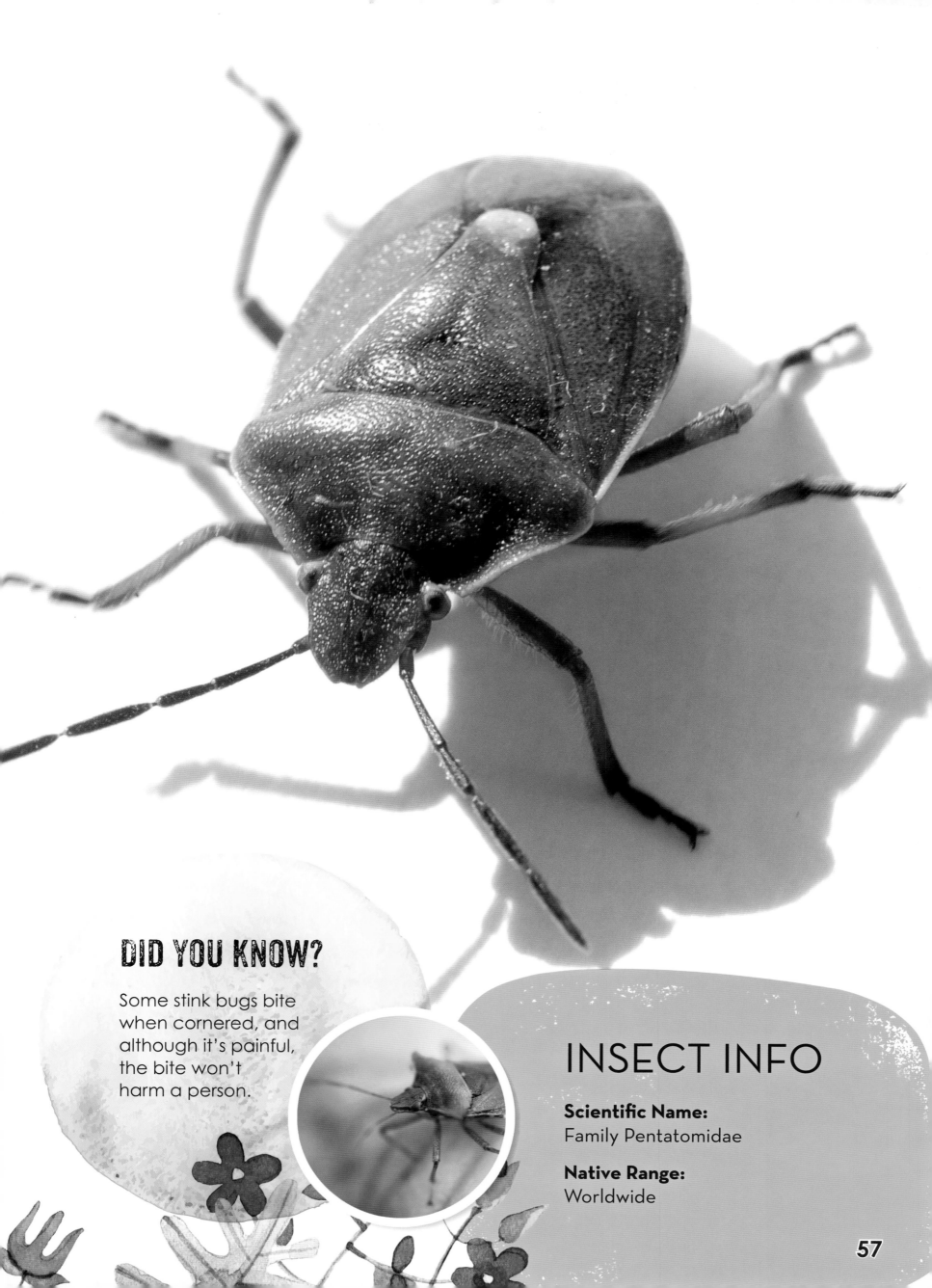

DID YOU KNOW?

Some stink bugs bite when cornered, and although it's painful, the bite won't harm a person.

INSECT INFO

Scientific Name:
Family Pentatomidae

Native Range:
Worldwide

INSECT INFO

Scientific Name:
Strategus aloeus

Native Range:
Florida to Arizona and
South America

DID YOU KNOW?

While some males have three large horns, others have smaller ones, and the females have no horns at all.

If you come upon a male ox beetle in the garden, you might scream and run in the other direction. That's because, at two inches long, this is one of the largest beetles in the United States. What's even scarier is that many male ox beetles have three horns jutting from behind their head!

As frightening as they may appear, ox beetles are gentle giants—some people keep them as pets and even play with them! They don't cause harm to anyone. Even their horns are used only to fight other males for a mate. In fact, ox beetles are welcomed as recyclers of Earth's debris.

THE GENTLE OX BEETLE

STINGING FIRE ANT

A large anthill could be a sign that fire ants are underfoot. Hundreds of thousands of ants can live in one colony. When their home is disturbed, ants pour out to attack. An intruder will likely be bitten and stung many times. These stings itch and burn, which is how fire ants got their name. Normally, the stings won't kill a human, but they'll kill the ants' favorite foods: ticks, insects, and worms.

Fire ants can live through near-freezing temperatures, droughts, and floods. Their waxy bodies keep them from drying out and helps them form a colony-size raft to float atop floodwaters.

INSECT INFO

Scientific Name:
Solenopsis invicta

Native Range:
South America

DID YOU KNOW?

Fire ants cost us billions of dollars a year for all the damage they do to us, livestock, crops, and irrigation and electrical systems.

DID YOU KNOW?

Earwigs got their name because people thought that earwigs would crawl into a person's ear to get to the brain and lay their eggs! Of course, this is not true.

INSECT INFO

Scientific Name:
Order Dermaptera

Native Range:
Worldwide except the Arctic and Antarctic

HIDING EARWIG

The long-bodied earwig is easy to recognize. Just take a look at the claw-like pincers on the rear end. Male pincers are curved, whereas a female's are straighter. The pincers are used for defense and for grasping prey. Earwigs eat mostly plants, damaging gardens and crops. But they also eat insects, such as aphids, that can be even more damaging to plants.

Earwig mothers are special in the insect world. Most insects lay eggs and leave the nest, but earwigs actually tend to their eggs and young. The mother moves the eggs around to keep them from getting moldy, and she helps feed her young.

INSECT INFO

Scientific Name:
Pelidnota punctata

Native Range:
Eastern to central
United States and
eastern Canada

DID YOU KNOW?

The grapevine beetle's
larvae can take as long
as two years to develop
into adults.

NIGHT-FLYING GRAPEVINE BEETLE

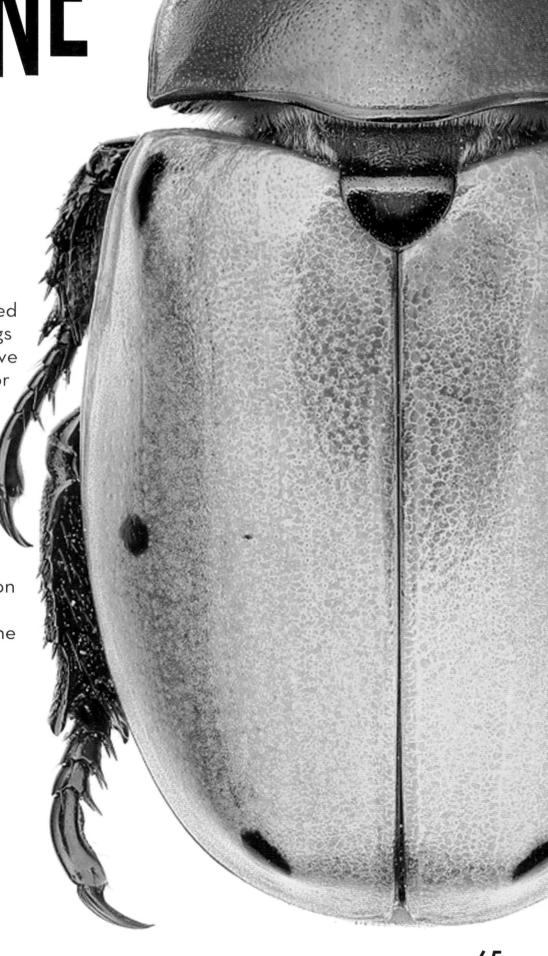

Often confused with a ladybug, the spotted yellow-orange beetle is bigger, and it hangs around grapevines. The beetle is also active at night, flying around to find grapevines or a mate. Its antennae have orange balls at their tips. These balls unroll to expose tiny plates that help grapevine beetles "smell" for food or a mate.

During the day, this pretty beetle just sits around on a grapevine leaf, which also happens to be its favorite food. Sometimes so many beetles are chewing on grapevines that they ruin a whole crop. That's how the grapevine beetle earned the reputation of being a pest.

THE PATIENT PRAYING MANTIS

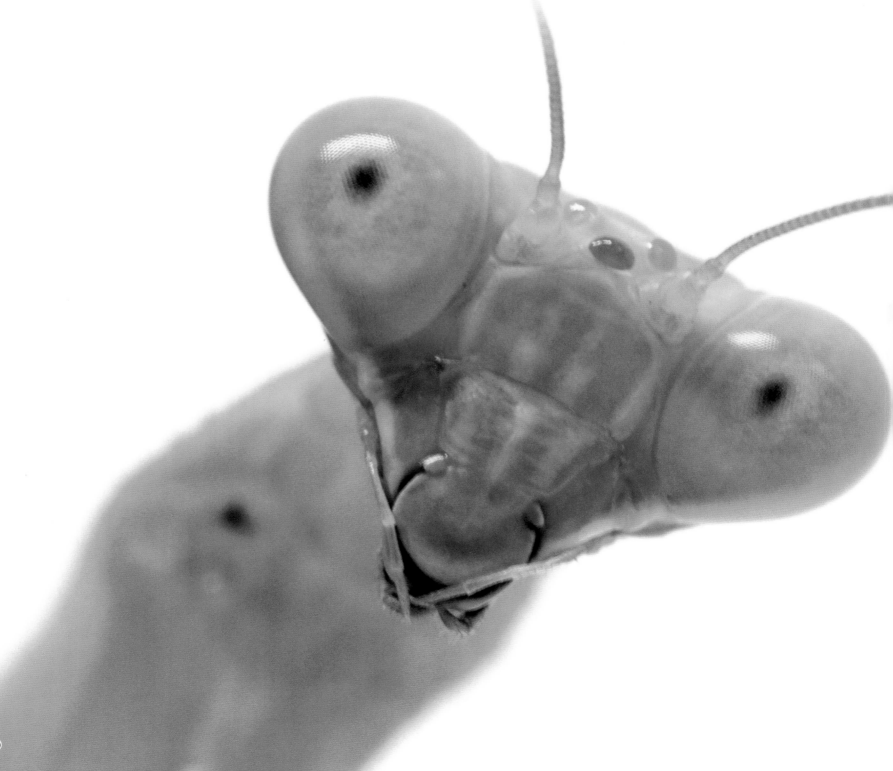

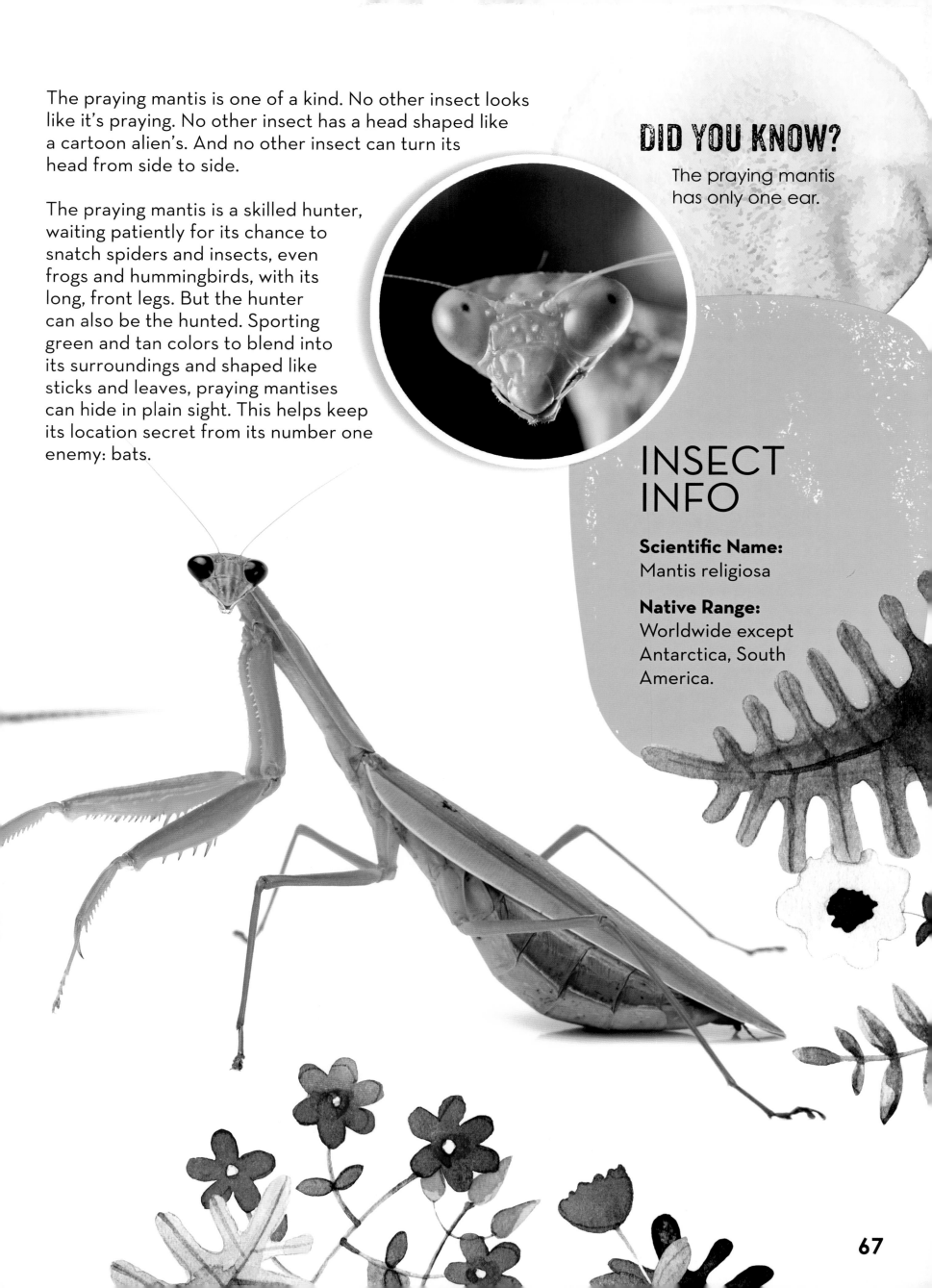

The praying mantis is one of a kind. No other insect looks like it's praying. No other insect has a head shaped like a cartoon alien's. And no other insect can turn its head from side to side.

The praying mantis is a skilled hunter, waiting patiently for its chance to snatch spiders and insects, even frogs and hummingbirds, with its long, front legs. But the hunter can also be the hunted. Sporting green and tan colors to blend into its surroundings and shaped like sticks and leaves, praying mantises can hide in plain sight. This helps keep its location secret from its number one enemy: bats.

DID YOU KNOW?

The praying mantis has only one ear.

INSECT INFO

Scientific Name:
Mantis religiosa

Native Range:
Worldwide except Antarctica, South America.

DID YOU KNOW?

A grasshopper's hind legs act like wound-up springs that thrust them into the air when they're released.

INSECT INFO

Scientific Name:
Dactylotum bicolor

Native Range:
Southern Canada, United States, and northern Mexico

Most grasshoppers are shades of brown and green to blend with their surroundings. But the rainbow grasshopper is so colorful, it catches the eye. The colors, though, advertise that this beauty tastes horrible and may be toxic. Even if it's not true, predators stay away. The rainbow grasshopper has another trait that's different from most other grasshoppers. It doesn't fly. It relies only on its strong hind legs to hop away from danger.

Many kinds of grasshoppers can do a lot of damage to crops. But even though the rainbow grasshopper munches on leaves, it hardly ever harms crops.

THE HARMLESS
RAINBOW GRASSHOPPER

THE DESTRUCTIVE JAPANESE BEETLE

The first Japanese beetles to arrive in the United States landed in New Jersey around 1912. These newcomers didn't have natural enemies in the United States, so their population spread throughout most of the country. Now, Japanese beetles are the most common lawn pest. The adults aren't to blame, though. It's their young, the larvae (also called grubs), that eat grass roots and turn a green backyard to brown. The adults are guilty of a different type of destruction. They prefer to eat the leaves of a variety of plants, munching them down to their skeletons.

INSECT INFO

Scientific Name:
Popillia japonica

Native Range:
Asia

Non-Native Range:
Canada, United States, Portugal, Russia, and China

DID YOU KNOW?

Adult Japanese beetles dine in groups on a variety of plants. They can strip the leaves of a peach tree in 15 minutes!

PARALYZING TARANTULA HAWK WASP

Tarantula hawk wasps don't have many enemies, but bullfrogs and roadrunners find them tasty.

INSECT INFO

Scientific Name:
Pepsis sp.

Native Range:
Every continent except Antarctica and Europe

At almost two inches long, this blue-black wasp with orange wings delivers a paralyzing sting. Luckily, these wasps normally do not sting people. But tarantulas have to watch out.

When it's time for this wasp to lay an egg, she goes on the hunt for a tarantula. When she finds one, she stings it with a venom that paralyzes the creature within seconds, and then she drags it into a burrow. She lays an egg on the tarantula, covers up the burrow, and leaves. Once hatched, the wasp larva feasts on the paralyzed tarantula until the larva is full grown.

HOVERING RUSTIC

INSECT INFO

Scientific Name:
Manduca rustica

Native Range:
Southern United States, Mexico, Central America, and South America

DID YOU KNOW?

Because the rustic sphinx moth is active at night, it relies on night-blooming flowers for its food.

SPHINX MOTH

The large and striking rustic sphinx moth looks showy, but against a tree trunk it all but disappears. And with a wingspan of up to six inches, it's as big as a human palm.

These moths are active at night and fly from flower to flower for their favorite meal of nectar. The sphinx moth is specially built to drink the nectar of long-throated flowers. Their powerful wings allow them to hover as their straw-like mouthparts reach down into a flower and suck up its sweet juice. This behavior is so much like a hummingbird's that the moth's nickname is hummingbird moth.

STINGING MARICOPA HARVESTER ANT

DID YOU KNOW?

The horned lizard loves eating Maricopa harvester ants and isn't hurt by their stings.

INSECT INFO

Scientific Name:
Pogonomyrmex maricopa

Native Range:
United States, Mexico, and Antarctica

The Maricopa harvester ant has the most painful sting of any insect. It actually stings like a bee, separating from its stinger and leaving it to continue pumping venom into its victim. These ants sting to protect their nest and themselves. The main job of a harvester ant, though, is to harvest, or collect seeds, which they bring back to the nest and store for future meals.

These ants also capture and eat other bugs. Their sting doesn't keep them safe from being eaten themselves. Spiders, other insects, birds, and reptiles are among the enemies these harvester ants need to watch out for.

HUNTING SIX-SPOTTED TIGER BEETLE

DID YOU KNOW?

The strong jaws of the six-spotted tiger beetle are equipped with teeth.

INSECT INFO

Scientific Name:
Cicindela sexgutatta

Native Range:
Southeastern Canada to eastern United States, except the Gulf Coast

This shiny green beetle with its long legs and big eyes spends its days hunting other insects on forest paths. Like a tiger, this beetle stalks its prey and uses the element of surprise to capture it. The prey doesn't stand a chance against this tiger beetle's strong jaws.

To keep predators away, the six-spotted tiger beetle squirts out a juice that smells terrible. This is a fast-running beetle who can also fly with speed. Its green color allows the six-spotted tiger beetle to rest on leaves unnoticed. Although it is called six-spotted, this beetle may have fewer than six spots or no spots at all.

AMAZING INSECTS

The facts about insects sometime seem stranger than anything we could ever imagine. There are ants that can make a raft with their bodies, beetles that use the Milky Way as a map, cockroaches that can live (for a while) without their heads, and cicadas that sing from their bellies. Who could make up all this stuff?

But no matter how crazy they seem, insects play a serious role in our world. They keep the earth clean by helping dead plants and animals decompose, or rot, and enrich the soil. They pollinate flowers so they grow into fruits, nuts, seeds, and vegetables. And they are food for other animals such as birds, lizards, and mammals such as chimpanzees, anteaters, and even people! And let's not forget that they decorate our world with amazing colors and jaw-dropping shapes.

So the next time you step outside, go exploring. See what kinds of insects you can find in your own backyard. With all the millions of insects that haven't been discovered yet, you might find an insect no one has ever seen before!